GW00360790

THIS BOOK IS FOR

_____

WITH LOVE FROM

_____

CONTENTS

CONTENTS

before I arrived

date pregnancy confirmed _____

due date _____

date of scans _____

_____

my parents' thoughts and feelings _____

_____

_____

_____

_____

_____

_____

_____

_____

_____

_____

_____

_____

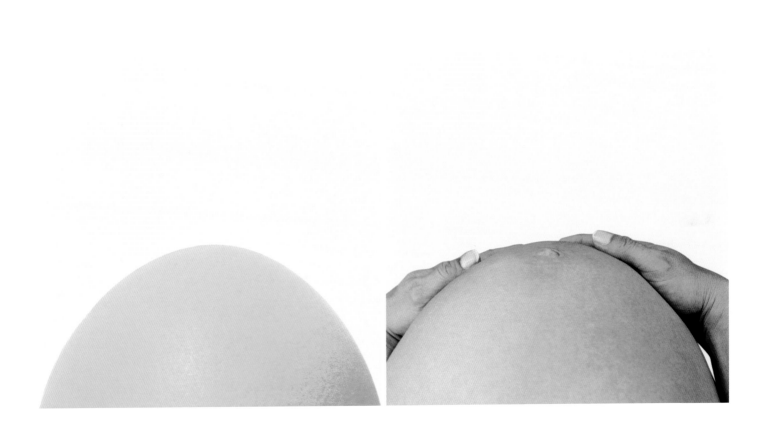

family and friends

Place photographs
of family, friends,
grandparents,
godparents.

grandmother

grandfather

grandmother

grandfather

mother

father

me

choosing my name

favourite names for a girl

_____

_____

_____

_____

_____

_____

favourite names for a boy

_____

_____

_____

_____

_____

_____

_____

my birth day

date _____ day of week _____

time _____

place of birth _____

name(s) of midwife/doctor _____

_____

who was present at the birth _____

_____

_____

_____

my weight _____ my length _____

hair colour _____ eye colour _____

blood type _____

my place in the family _____

_____

_____

star sign _____

birth stone _____

_____

your photos here

date I came home

address of our family home

how my parents felt

home at last

birth announcement
birth certificate
hospital tag
gift cards

my first visitors

Place photographs
of baby at home with
family and friends.
Add any special messages.

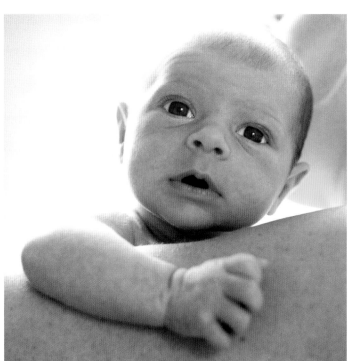

your photos here

my naming ceremony

my full name
_____

what my name means
_____
_____

why it was chosen
_____
_____
_____

my nickname
_____
_____

date of ceremony/christening
_____

venue
_____

name of celebrant
_____

names of godparents
_____
_____

who was there
_____
_____
_____
_____
_____

sleeping

first time I slept through the night

_____

_____

_____

_____

my favourite bedtime stories/lullabies

_____

_____

_____

my favourite bedtime toys

_____

_____

_____

_____

_____

_____

date I was weaned from the breast/bottle

first pureed food I ever tasted

first fingerfood I ever tasted

my favourite food

my least favourite food

first held a spoon

first held a cup

bathtime

my favourite water games

_____
_____
_____
_____
_____
_____

my favourite bath toys

_____
_____
_____
_____
_____
_____
_____
_____

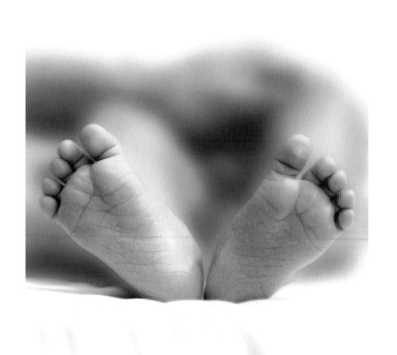

early days (3 months)

where we live

_____

_____

_____

_____

what I am like

_____

_____

_____

_____

_____

_____

_____

_____

_____

_____

what makes me happy

_____

_____

_____

_____

_____

_____

_____

what is happening in my world

_____

_____

_____

_____

_____

_____

_____

_____

your photos here

what I can do now

what sounds I make

my favourite foods

_____

_____

_____

_____

_____

_____

my favourite toys

_____

_____

_____

_____

_____

_____

_____

_____

your photos here

early days (9 months)

what I am like

_____

_____

_____

_____

_____

_____

_____

what is happening in my world

_____

_____

_____

_____

_____

_____

_____

_____

_____

my favourite foods

_____

_____

_____

_____

_____

_____

my favourite toys

_____

_____

_____

_____

_____

_____

_____

lock of hair [place in envelope]

your photos here

hand prints

Left   Right

footprints

Left

Right

where we celebrated

_____

_____

_____

who was there

_____

_____

_____

special gifts

_____

_____

_____

_____

birthday cake

_____

_____

_____

your photos here

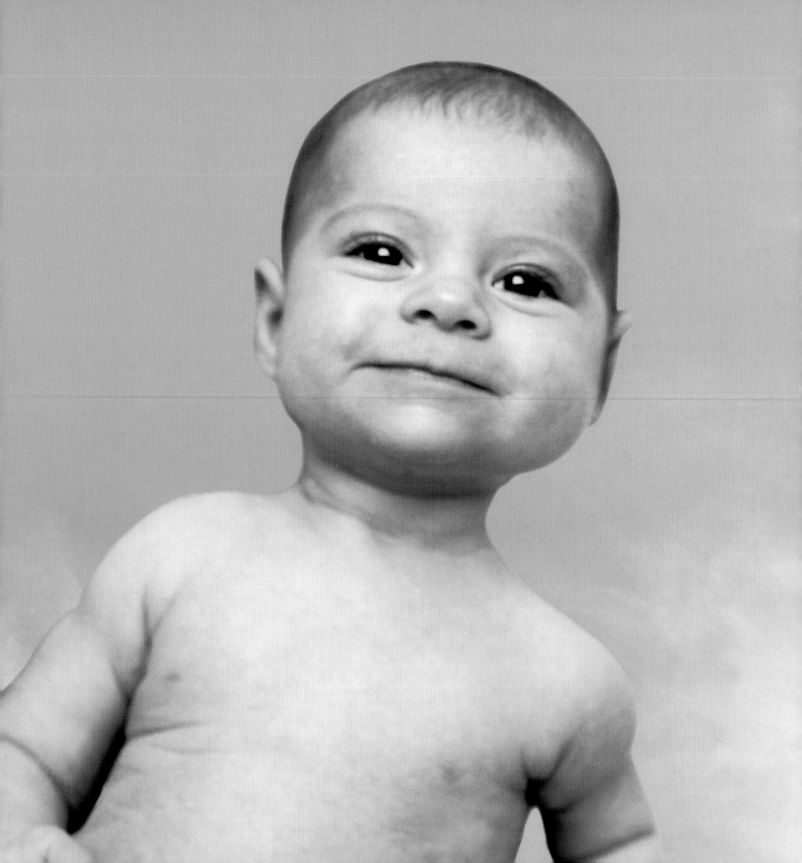

now i'm one

what I love doing

who my friends are

words I can say

my favourite games

health

blood type _____

allergies _____

other _____

_____

_____

_____

_____

_____

_____

_____

_____

_____

_____

height and weight

age	weight	height
1 month		
2 months		
3 months		
4 months		
5 months		
6 months		
7 months		
8 months		
9 months		
10 months		
11 months		
12 months		

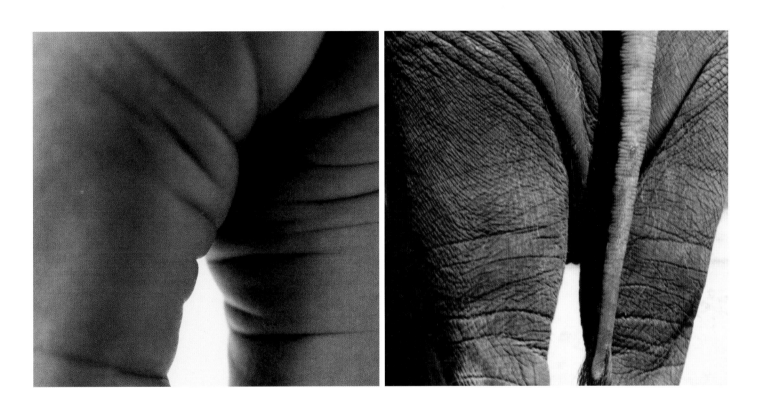

where we celebrated

_____

_____

_____

_____

who was there

_____

_____

_____

_____

my favourite gifts

_____

_____

_____

_____

_____

_____

Place photographs of
Christmas Day celebrations,
decorations, friends and family.

your photos here

special friends

Place photographs
of special friends,
pets and favourite toys.

happy moments

sad moments

my first teeth

Date: _____

_____

_____

_____

_____

_____

upper

Date: _____

_____

_____

_____

_____

_____

Date: _____

_____

_____

_____

_____

lower

Date: _____

_____

_____

_____

_____

holidays and travel

your photos here

your photos here

funny moments

where we celebrated

who was there

special gifts

birthday cake

your photos here

your photos here

my third birthday

where we celebrated

_____

_____

_____

who was there

_____

_____

_____

special gifts

_____

_____

_____

_____

birthday cake

_____

_____

_____

where we celebrated

_____

_____

_____

who was there

_____

_____

_____

special gifts

_____

_____

_____

_____

birthday cake

_____

_____

_____

your photos here

your photos here

where we celebrated

_____

_____

_____

_____

who was there

_____

_____

_____

_____

special gifts

_____

_____

_____

_____

birthday cake

_____

_____

_____

my first paintings/drawings

messages for the future

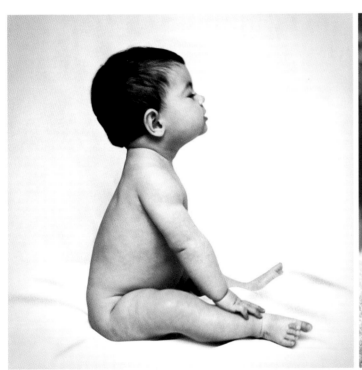

First of all I would like to thank Emeric Dubois for his advice, my agent Véronique Roc, my assistant Valérie Quemener and Guillaume Mollet.

I would also like to thank all the dogs and their masters: Athena and the Orgeval SPA, the Animal Center at Chambourcy for their kindness and the great work with the puppies, the Thoiry Zoo and its wolf cubs, Stéphane Delhez of the Bonnières kennel and cattery for the labradors, great dane, bulldog and cocker spaniel, Véronique Valy and her kennels Chevaloupsgreg, little Haras at Port Mort for the Eurasiers, the husky and the Siberian husky, Mrs Parsy-Thobois of the Balines dog breeding centre for the basset hound, the Cairns terrier and the cocker spaniel, Verneuil animal grooming, Mrs Franca and Youpi, Mrs Duminy of the "Au chien royal" grooming salon at Neuilly for the grey standard poodle, Mrs Mesnil Christiane of Grand Chelem and Rocco the boxer, Sylvie Legivre of Domaine de Lutèce and Ushuaia the Mâtin de Naples, Mr Legivre and Syrius the Mâtin de Naples, Francine Clesse of Tchesskaia for the Borzois, the Cavalier King Charles spaniels, Mrs Rohmer and Siska the dalmatian, Caroline Grobost and her French bulldog, Mr and Mrs Silva-Bourdin and Tito the Jack Russel, Astrid and Colette the Rottweiler, Pascaline for her West Highland and her Scottish terriers, Mrs Liotte for her German Spitz and Mrs Le Saulnier for her Yorkshire terrier.

Of course I also thank the following babies for their kind participation: Aleksi, Alicia, Benjamin, Chloé, Cyprien, the twins Faustin and Oscar, Gabriel, Inés, Jeanne, Lalou, Lena, the twins Léo and Sacha, Lesly, Lyderick, Mathis, Mathy, Noemi, Noham, Sharleyne, Tanguy, Théo, Thibault and Tony.

Vicky Ceelen

Published by **The Five Mile Press.**
950 Stud Road, Rowville 3178 Victoria, Australia
Email: publishing@fivemile.com.au
Website: www.fivemile.com.au

Copyright © 2005 Editions Hors Collection

This edition first published 2005
Published in association with PQ Publishers Limited, 116 Symonds Street,
Auckland, New Zealand

No part of this publication may be reproduced (except brief passages for the
purpose of review), stored in a retrieval system or transmitted in any form by
any means, electronic, mechanical, photocopying, recording or otherwise,
without the prior written permission of the publisher.

The original publisher is grateful for permission to reproduce the following
item subject to copyright. Every effort has been made to trace the copyright
holders and the publisher apologises for any unintentional omission. We
would be pleased to hear from any not acknowledged here and undertake to
make all reasonable efforts to include the appropriate acknowledgement in
any subsequent editions.

Designed by Kylie Nicholls.
Printed by Midas Printing International Limited, China.

ISBN 1 7412 4556 7